ORIGAMI SAFARI

Grassland Animals

By Ruth Owen

WINDMILL BOOKS™

New York

Published in 2015 by Windmill Books, An Imprint of Rosen Publishing
29 East 21st Street, New York, NY 10010

First Edition

Produced for Rosen by Ruby Tuesday Books Ltd
Editor for Ruby Tuesday Books Ltd: Mark J. Sachner
US Editor: Joshua Shadowens
Designer: Emma Randall

Photo Credits:
Cover, 1, 3, 5, 6–7, 8–9, 10–11, 12–13, 14–15, 16–17, 18–19, 20–21, 22–23, 24–25, 26–27, 28–29, 31 © Ruby Tuesday Books; cover, 4–5, 6, 10, 14, 18, 22, 26 © Shutterstock.

Library of Congress Cataloging-in-Publication Data

Owen, Ruth, 1967– author.
 Grassland animals / by Ruth Owen. — First Edition.
    pages cm. — (Origami safari)
 Includes index.
 ISBN 978-1-4777-9253-7 (library binding) —
 ISBN 978-1-4777-9254-4 (pbk.) — ISBN 978-1-4777-9255-1 (6-pack)
 1. Origami—Juvenile literature. 2. Grassland animals in art—Juvenile literature. 3. Animals in art—Juvenile literature. I. Title.
 TT872.5.O934 2015
 736.982—dc23
                                             2014013963

Manufactured in the United States of America

CPSIA Compliance Information: Batch #WS14WM: For Further Information contact Rosen Publishing, New York, New York at 1-866-478-0556

Contents

Grassland Origami

Grasslands are a type of wild **habitat**. These open areas of land are covered with grass, low-growing bushes, and just a few trees.

The grasslands of Africa are hot and dry for about six to eight months of the year. This dry season is then followed by heavy rains during the wet season.

Many different animals live on Africa's grasslands. In this book you can read about six African grassland animals. You will also get the chance to make a fantastic **origami** model of each animal.

All you need is some paper, and you will be ready to follow the step-by-step instructions to make your own collection of origami animals.

Grassland
in Africa

Origami! Elephant

Elephants aren't just the largest animals that live on the grasslands of Africa. They are the largest land animals in the world.

Elephants live in small **herds** of adult females and their young. The youngsters range from tiny babies to teenagers. The leader of the herd is called the **matriarch**. She is the oldest and smartest member of the group. Adult male, or bull, elephants mostly live alone.

Elephants spend hours each day looking for food and water. They eat leaves, branches, tree bark, roots, grass, fruit, and seeds. They use their **trunks** to pull up clumps of grass or to pull tree branches to their mouths.

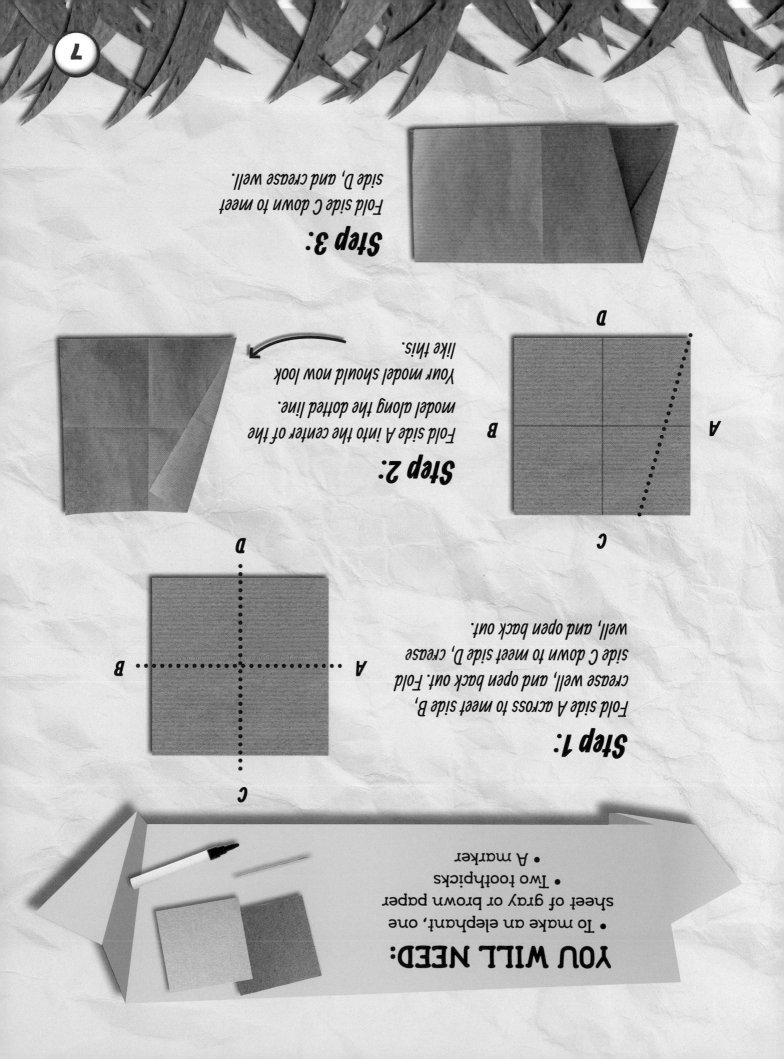

YOU WILL NEED:

- To make an elephant, one sheet of gray or brown paper
- Two toothpicks
- A marker

Step 1:

Fold side A across to meet side B, crease well, and open back out. Fold side C down to meet side D, crease well, and open back out.

Step 2:

Fold side A into the center of the model along the dotted line. Your model should now look like this.

Step 3:

Fold side C down to meet side D, and crease well.

Step 6:
Now gently squash down the open part of the model, and crease well so that the model is flat.

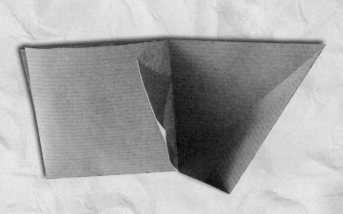

Step 5:
Now open out the folds you've made on the left-hand side of the model.

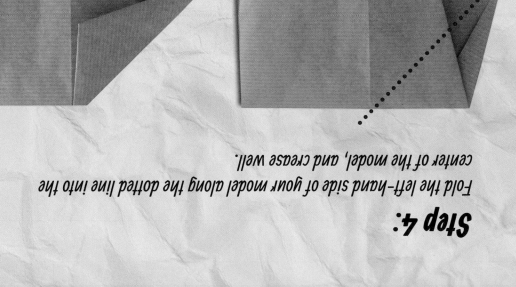

Step 4:
Fold the left-hand side of your model along the dotted line into the center of the model, and crease well.

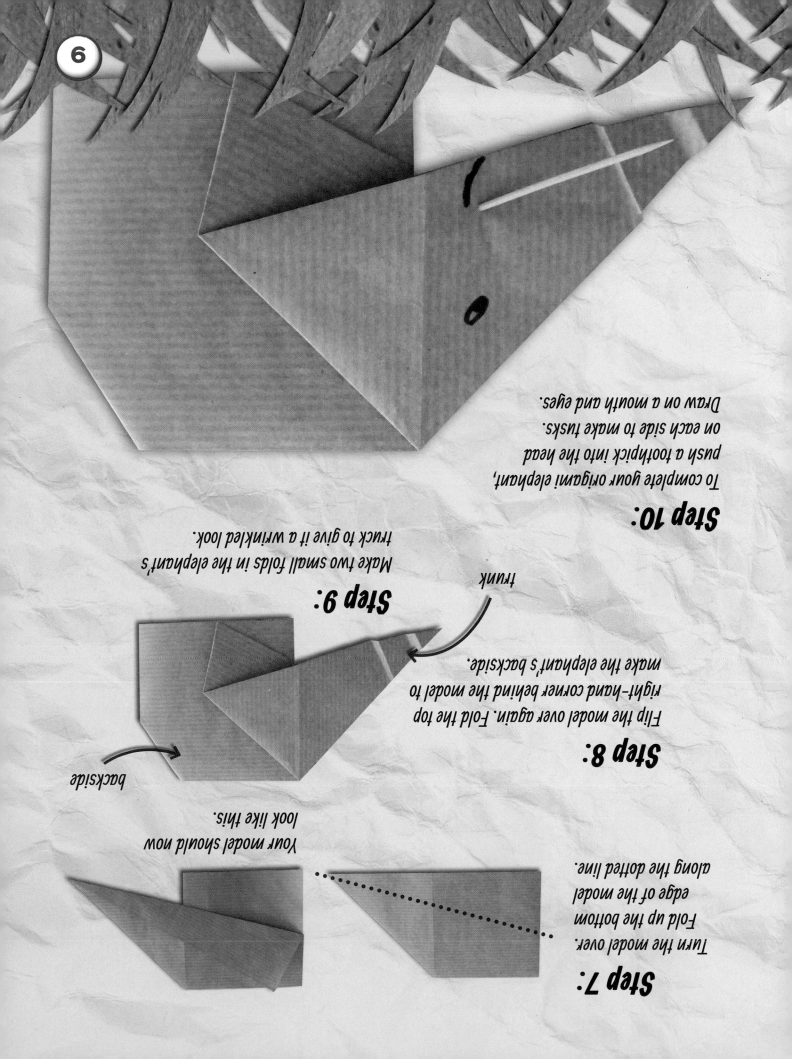

Step 10:

To complete your origami elephant, push a toothpick into the head on each side to make tusks. Draw on a mouth and eyes.

Step 9:

Make two small folds in the elephant's trunk to give it a wrinkled look.

trunk

Step 8:

Flip the model over again. Fold the top right-hand corner behind the model to make the elephant's backside.

backside

Your model should now look like this.

Step 7:

Turn the model over. Fold up the bottom edge of the model along the dotted line.

Origami Giraffe

Giraffes are the towering giants of Africa's grasslands. An adult male giraffe can grow to be 19 feet (5.8 m) tall. Even a newborn giraffe calf is about 6 feet (1.8 m) tall!

Giraffes eat leaves and twigs from acacia trees. These trees grow sharp thorns to protect themselves from being eaten by hungry grassland animals. The thorns don't bother giraffes, however. A giraffe's super-long, leathery tongue can twist and turn between the thorns to grab the leaves.

Giraffes are too large for most grassland **predators** to attack. Lions and crocodiles may kill an adult giraffe, though. To defend themselves, giraffes kick with their huge hooves, or run away at up to 35 miles per hour (56 km/h).

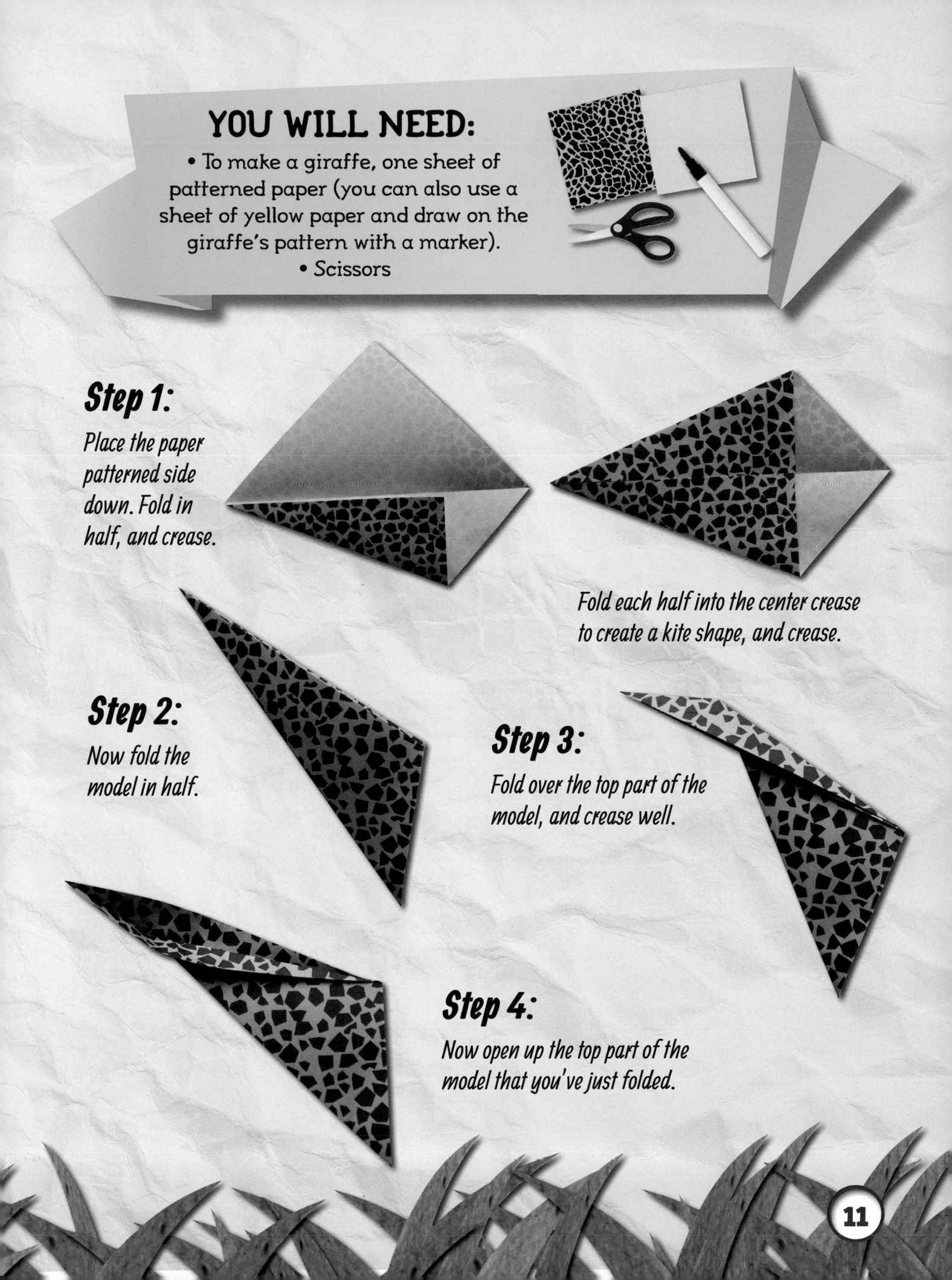

YOU WILL NEED:

• To make a giraffe, one sheet of patterned paper (you can also use a sheet of yellow paper and draw on the giraffe's pattern with a marker).
• Scissors

Step 1:

Place the paper patterned side down. Fold in half, and crease.

Fold each half into the center crease to create a kite shape, and crease.

Step 2:

Now fold the model in half.

Step 3:

Fold over the top part of the model, and crease well.

Step 4:

Now open up the top part of the model that you've just folded.

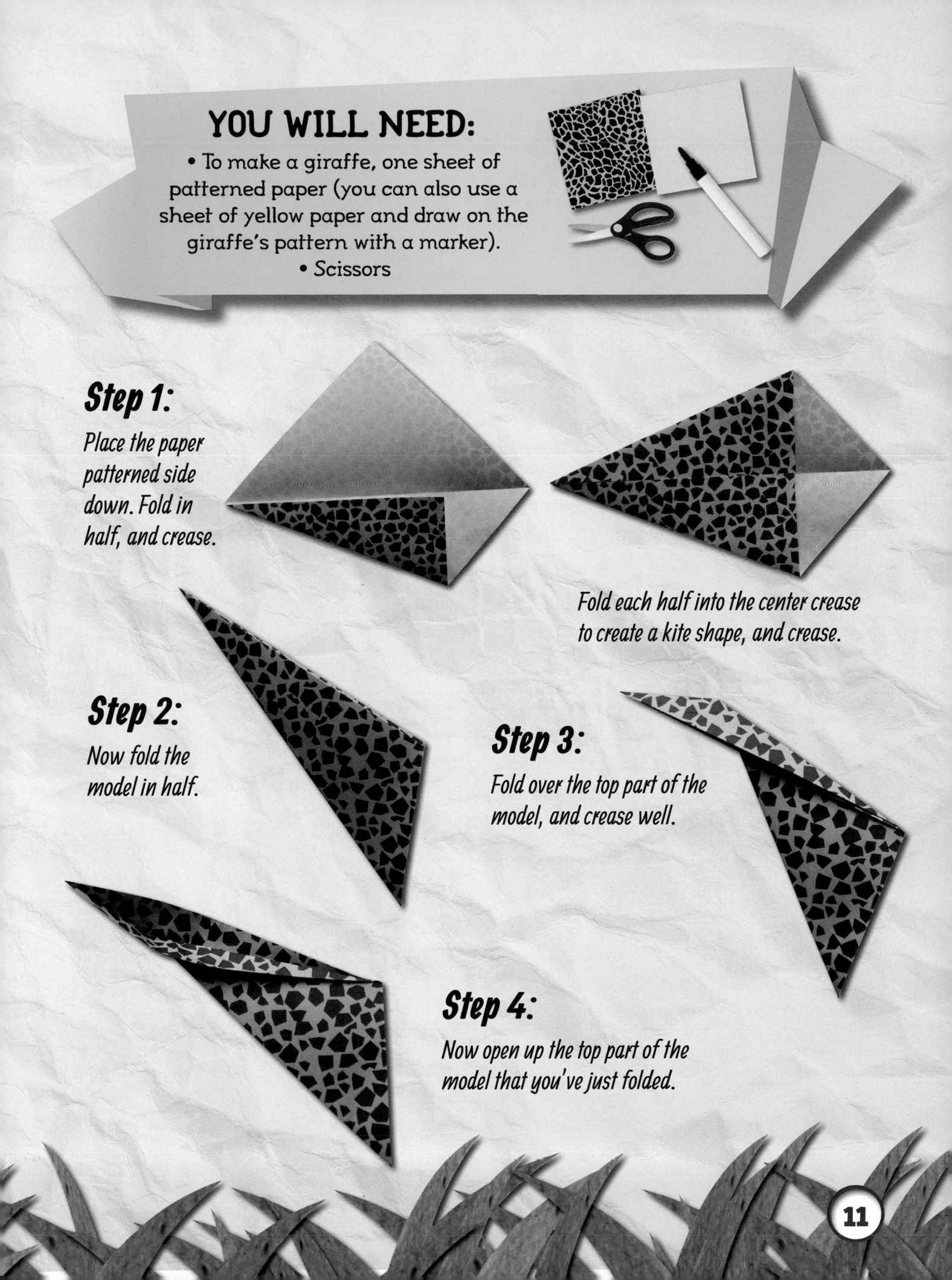

11

Step 5:

Take hold of point A and gently fold it backward.

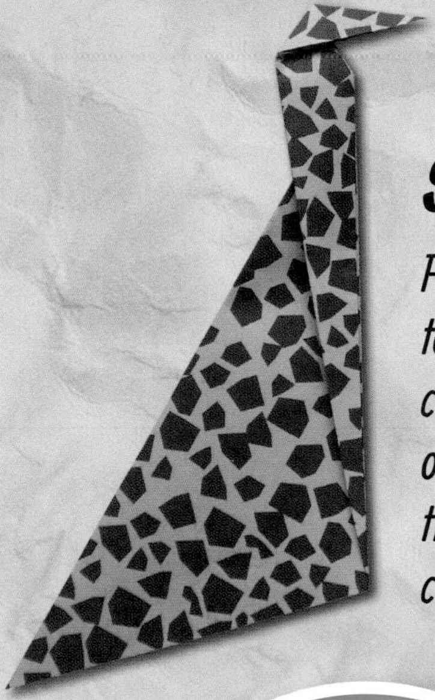

Step 6:

Fold the top point of the model to create the giraffe's head, crease, and then unfold. Open out the giraffe's neck and fold the head forward, using the creases you've just made.

The giraffe's head should now look like this.

Step 7:

Tuck the point inside the head to square off the giraffe's nose.

Step 8:

Now fold the left-hand side of the model toward the right-hand side, and crease. Then fold the point back toward the left so that it overlaps the edge of the model to create the giraffe's tail.

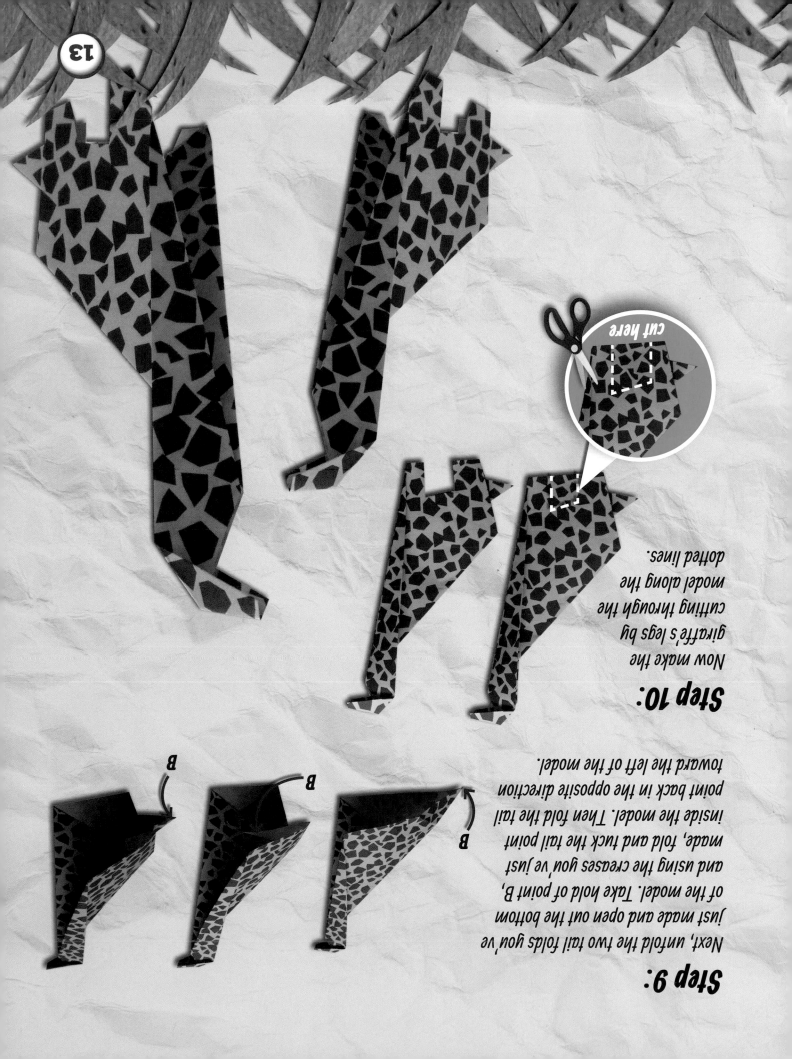

cut here

Step 10:
Now make the giraffe's legs by cutting through the model along the dotted lines.

Step 9:
Next, unfold the two tail folds you've just made and open out the bottom of the model. Take hold of point B, and using the creases you've just made, fold and tuck the tail point inside the model. Then fold the tail point back in the opposite direction toward the left of the model.

B

B

B

Origami Zebra

Zebras are wild, striped members of the horse family. These black and white grassland animals live in herds and feed on grass.

Every zebra has its own **unique** pattern of stripes. When zebras are **grazing** together as a large group, the stripes help them confuse lions, leopards, and other predators. The zebras' patterns blur together, making it hard for a predator to pick out one animal from the herd to attack.

A zebra foal learns its mother's pattern of stripes soon after it is born. This allows the baby to follow its mother and be able to find her among all the other zebras in the herd.

YOU WILL NEED:

- To make a zebra, one sheet of black and white striped paper.
- You can also use a sheet of white paper and draw on black stripes with a marker.

Step 1:
Place the paper striped side down. Fold in half diagonally, and crease.

Step 2:
Now fold points A and B into the center crease to create a diamond-like shape. Crease well.

Fold each half into the center crease to create a kite shape, and crease.

Step 3:
Take hold of point A and open up the fold to create a pocket. Then gently squash the pocket down to create a new point.

Repeat on the other side with point B.

Step 4:

Turn the model over. Fold point D up to meet point C, and crease well.

C

D

Step 5:

To make the zebra's neck, fold the left-hand side of the model upward, and crease.

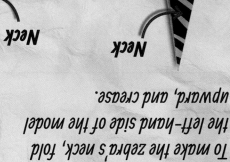

Neck

Body

Neck

Body

Next, unfold the crease you've just made. Open out the model at the top to create the two sides of the zebra's body. Then take the left-hand side of the model again and make a reverse, or backward, fold so that the neck tucks back between the two sides of the body.

Neck

Reverse fold

Body

Body

Gently flatten the model.

Step 6:

Fold over the top part of the neck to create the zebra's head, and crease.

Unfold the crease you've just made. Gently open out the head section and make a reverse fold by tucking the nose tip downward.

Tuck the point of the head backward into the head to create a square nose.

Step 7:

Take hold of the triangular flap on the side of the model and open it toward the zebra's head to create a front leg. Repeat on the other side of the model.

Front leg

Step 8:

Fold down the right-hand side of the model to create the zebra's back legs, and crease hard.

Step 9:

Fold the front leg back toward the right-hand side of the model along the dotted line, and crease hard. Repeat on the other side of the model.

Step 10:

Fold the zebra's neck back toward the right-hand side of the model, and crease hard. Repeat on the other side.

Step 11:

Turn the model over. Fold up the point of the zebra's back legs so that they are level with the front legs, and crease hard. Tuck the point into the zebra's body.

Origami Lion

Lions are one of the African grasslands' top predators. These big cats hunt animals such as zebras, antelope, wildebeest, and warthogs.

African lions live in family groups called **prides**. A pride is made up of an adult male, several adult females, young lions, and cubs.

Adult male lions can grow to be 10 feet (3 m) long, including their tails. They can weigh up to 530 pounds (240 kg). A male lion has a thick mane of hair that helps him look large and **impressive** when fighting other males. The mane also helps protect the lion's head and neck during fights.

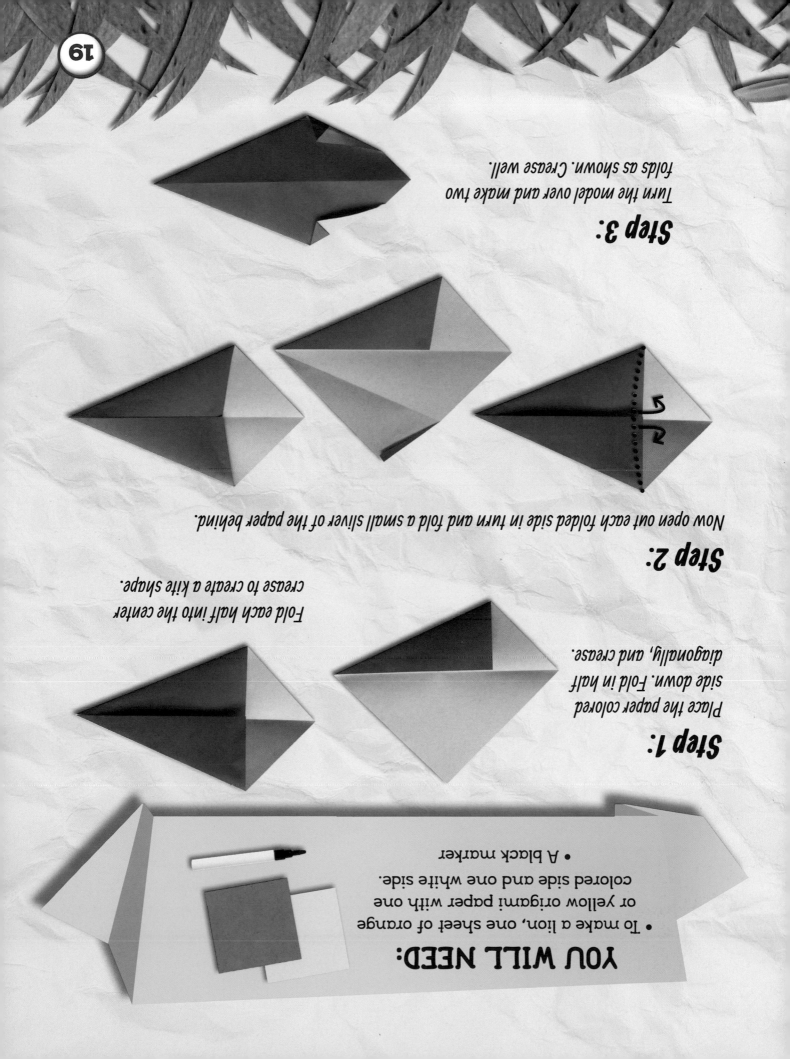

YOU WILL NEED:

- To make a lion, one sheet of orange or yellow origami paper with one colored side and one white side.
- A black marker

Step 1:
Place the paper colored side down. Fold in half diagonally, and crease.

Fold each half into the center crease to create a kite shape.

Step 2:
Now open out each folded side in turn and fold a small sliver of the paper behind.

Step 3:
Turn the model over and make two folds as shown. Crease well.

Step 4:

Fold point B up to meet point A, and crease well.

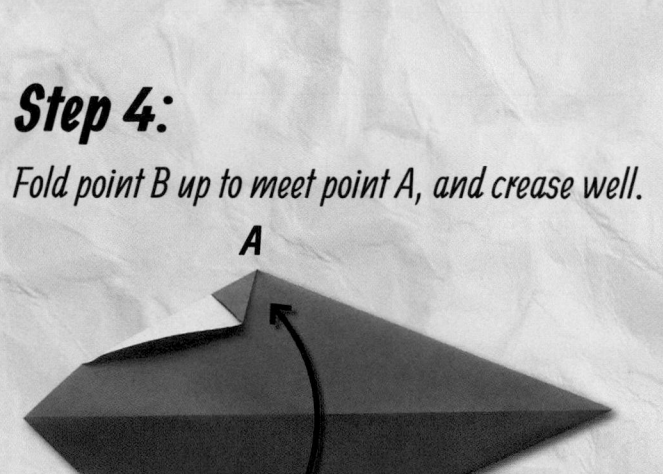

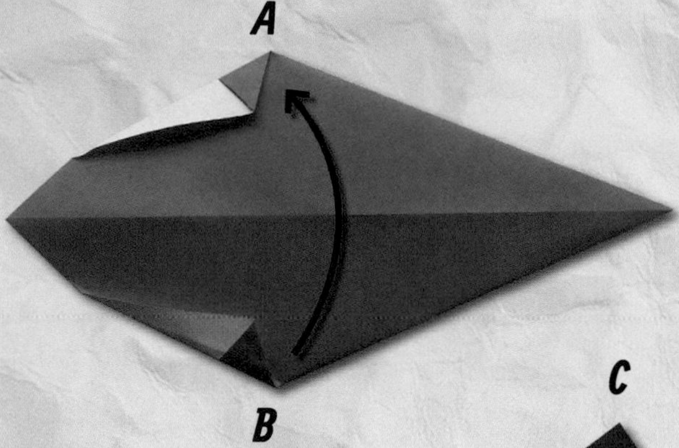

A

B

Step 5:

Open the model back out. Now gently begin to pull point C backward toward point D. You need to gently create folds as marked by the dotted lines.

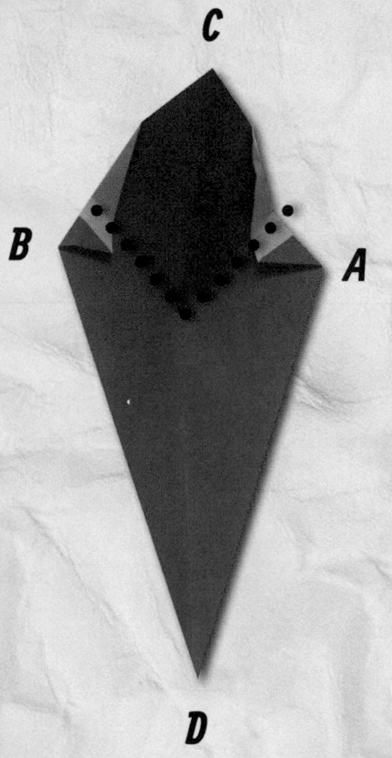

C

B

A

D

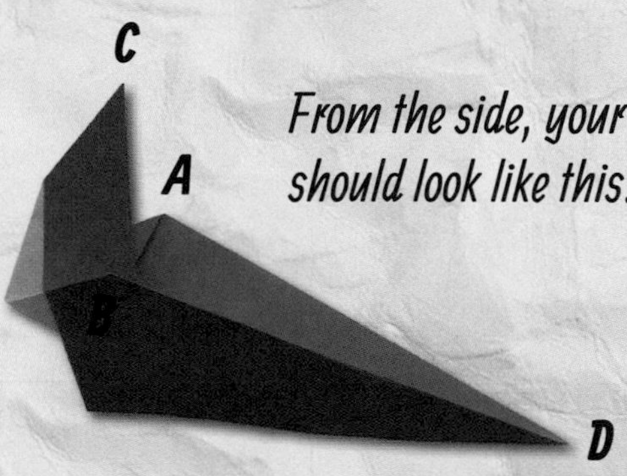

C

A

B

From the side, your model should look like this.

D

Gently squeeze and flatten the folds until your model looks like this.

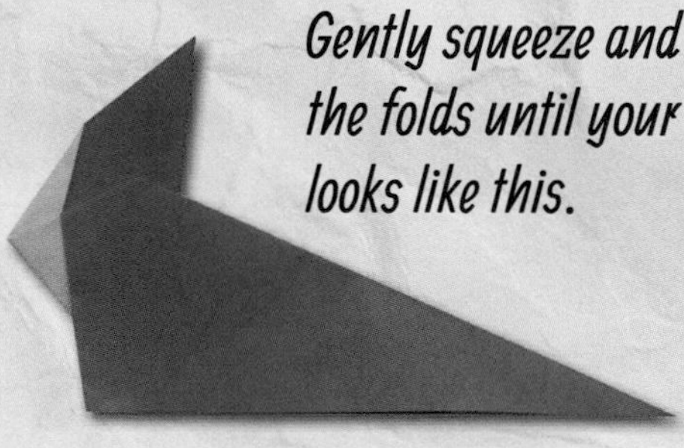

Step 6:

Now take hold of point E and open out the model.

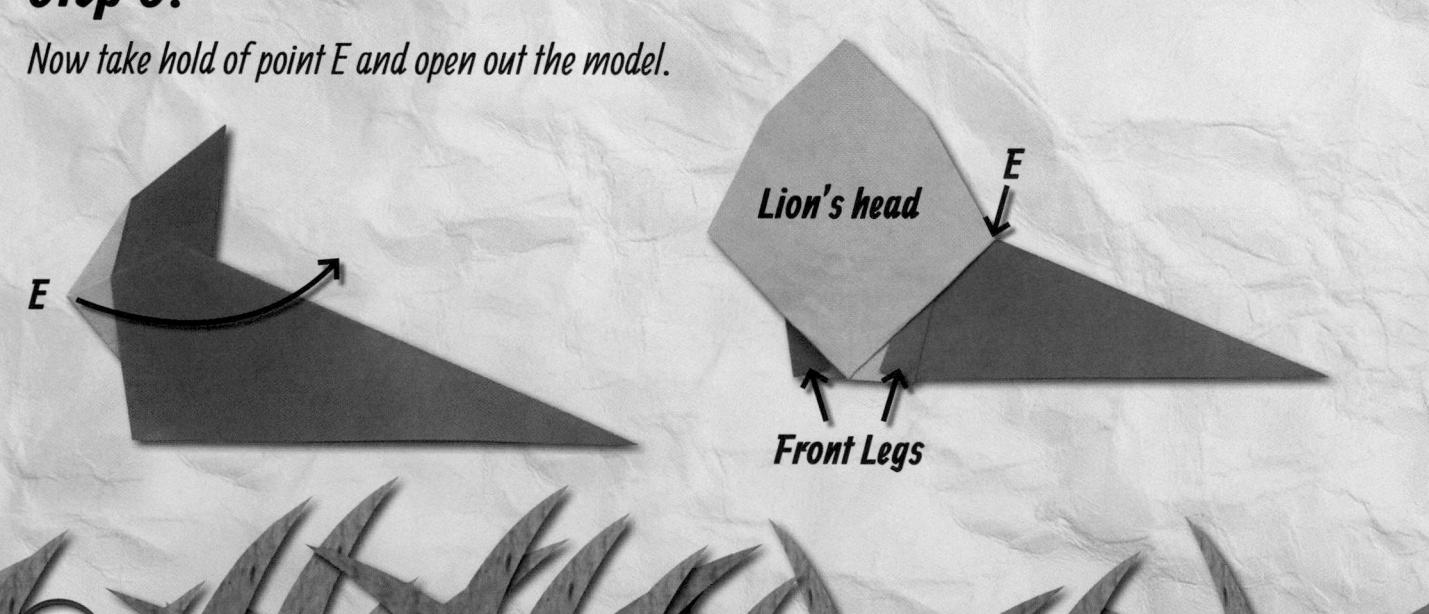

E

E

Lion's head

Front Legs

20

Step 7:
Fold down the top of the head to create the lion's face. Then tuck the bottom point of the face behind to create the lion's chin.

Step 8:
Fold the right-hand point of the model across the lion's body and face.

Step 9:
Then fold the point down to create the lion's tail.

Step 10:
Finally, open out the tail and add a final fold to help steady the lion. Draw the lion's face using a marker.

Origami Warthog

Warthogs are wild members of the pig family. They have wart-like growths on their faces and curved **tusks**. An adult warthog's tusks might grow to be 2 feet (61 cm) long.

Female warthogs live in groups with their piglets. Adult male warthogs usually live alone. Warthogs spend their days grazing on grass. They sometimes use their snouts and tusks to dig for underground plant parts such as **bulbs** and roots.

At night, warthogs sleep in **burrows**. They don't dig their own underground homes, but use natural holes in the ground. Often they move into an empty burrow that once belonged to another animal, such as an aardvark.

YOU WILL NEED:
- To make a warthog, one sheet of origami paper
- A toothpick
- A marker

Step 1:
Place the paper white or plain side down. Fold in half, and crease.

Step 2:
Now fold the top half of the paper back on itself, creating an accordion fold.

Turn the model over and fold down the other side, making another accordion fold.

Step 3:
Take hold of corner A and fold it down along the dotted line. You should only be folding the top layer of paper. Crease well and then unfold.

A

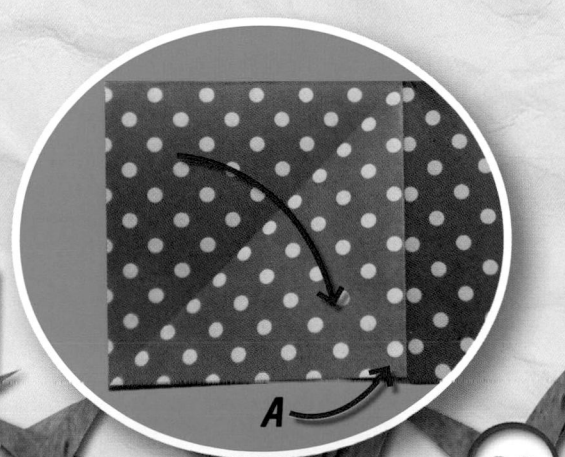

Step 4:

Now fold the end of the model along the dotted line, and crease. Then unfold.

Step 5:

Now lift up the bottom left-hand corner of the model to create a pocket. Using the creases you made in steps 3 and 4, gently squeeze and flatten the pocket to make a triangle.

Pocket

Triangle

Pocket

Step 6:

Now repeat steps 3, 4, and 5 at the right-hand end of the model.

Then turn the model over and repeat steps 3, 4, and 5 at both ends.

Your model should now look like this.

Step 7:

Now take the inside point of one triangle and fold it over and down to create the warthog's leg.

Repeat on the other three triangles.

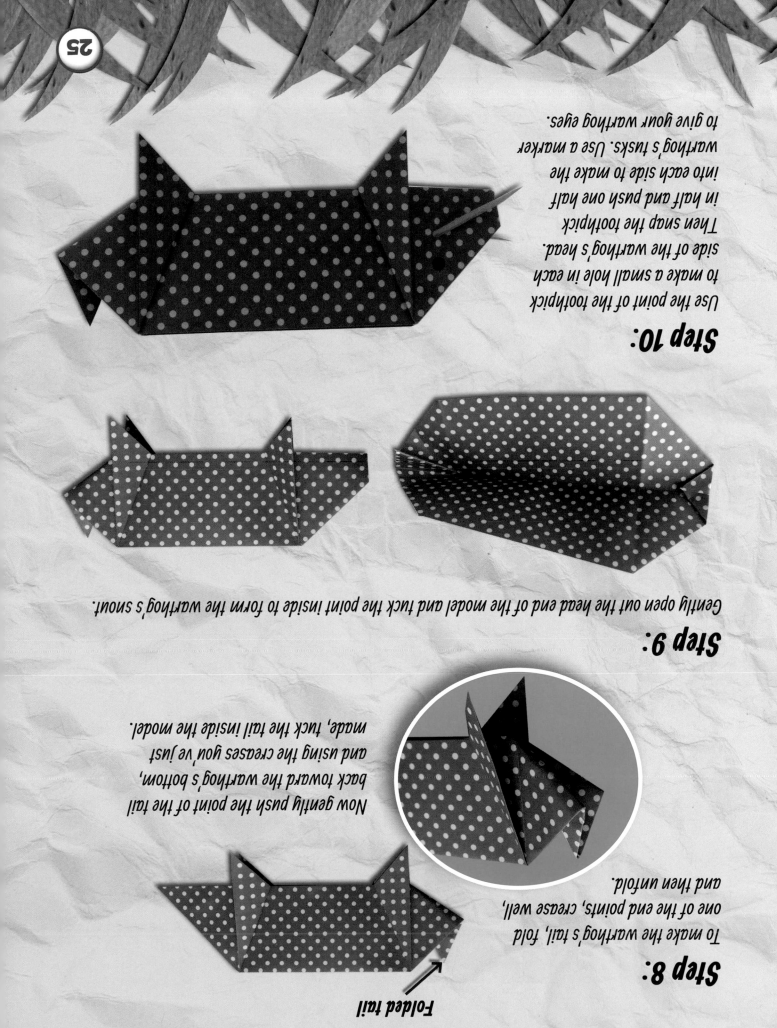

Step 8:
To make the warthog's tail, fold one of the end points, crease well, and then unfold.

Now gently push the point of the tail back toward the warthog's bottom, and using the creases you've just made, tuck the tail inside the model.

Folded tail

Step 9:
Gently open out the head end of the model and tuck the point inside to form the warthog's snout.

Step 10:
Use the point of the toothpick to make a small hole in each side of the warthog's head. Then snap the toothpick in half and push one half into each side to make the warthog's tusks. Use a marker to give your warthog eyes.

Origami Crocodile

Crocodiles are huge **reptiles** that have been on Earth for more than 200 million years. An adult male crocodile may grow to be 20 feet (6 m) long!

Crocodiles spend their lives in water and on riverbanks. They can float at the water's surface, or spend up to an hour underwater—without taking a breath!

Crocodiles catch and eat any grassland creature that comes close. They eat small **prey** such as fish, turtles, birds, and monkeys. They also catch and eat large animals such as wildebeest, zebra, and even giraffes. Crocodiles don't chew their food. They bite off large chunks of meat with their powerful jaws and then swallow them whole.

YOU WILL NEED:

- To make a crocodile, one sheet of origami paper
- A marker

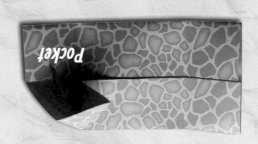

Step 1:

Place the paper patterned or colored side down. Fold the paper in half, crease, and then unfold. Next, fold each half into the center, and crease well.

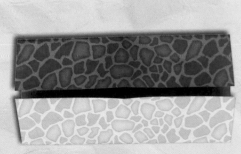

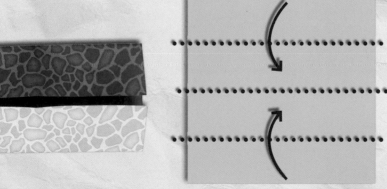

Step 2:

Now fold the ends of the model into the center to make a square, crease well, and then unfold both ends.

Step 3:

Now lift up the top right-hand corner of the model to create a pocket. Using the creases you made in steps 1 and 2, gently squeeze and flatten the pocket to make a triangle.

Pocket

Pocket

Step 4:

Repeat step 3 on the other three corners of the model.

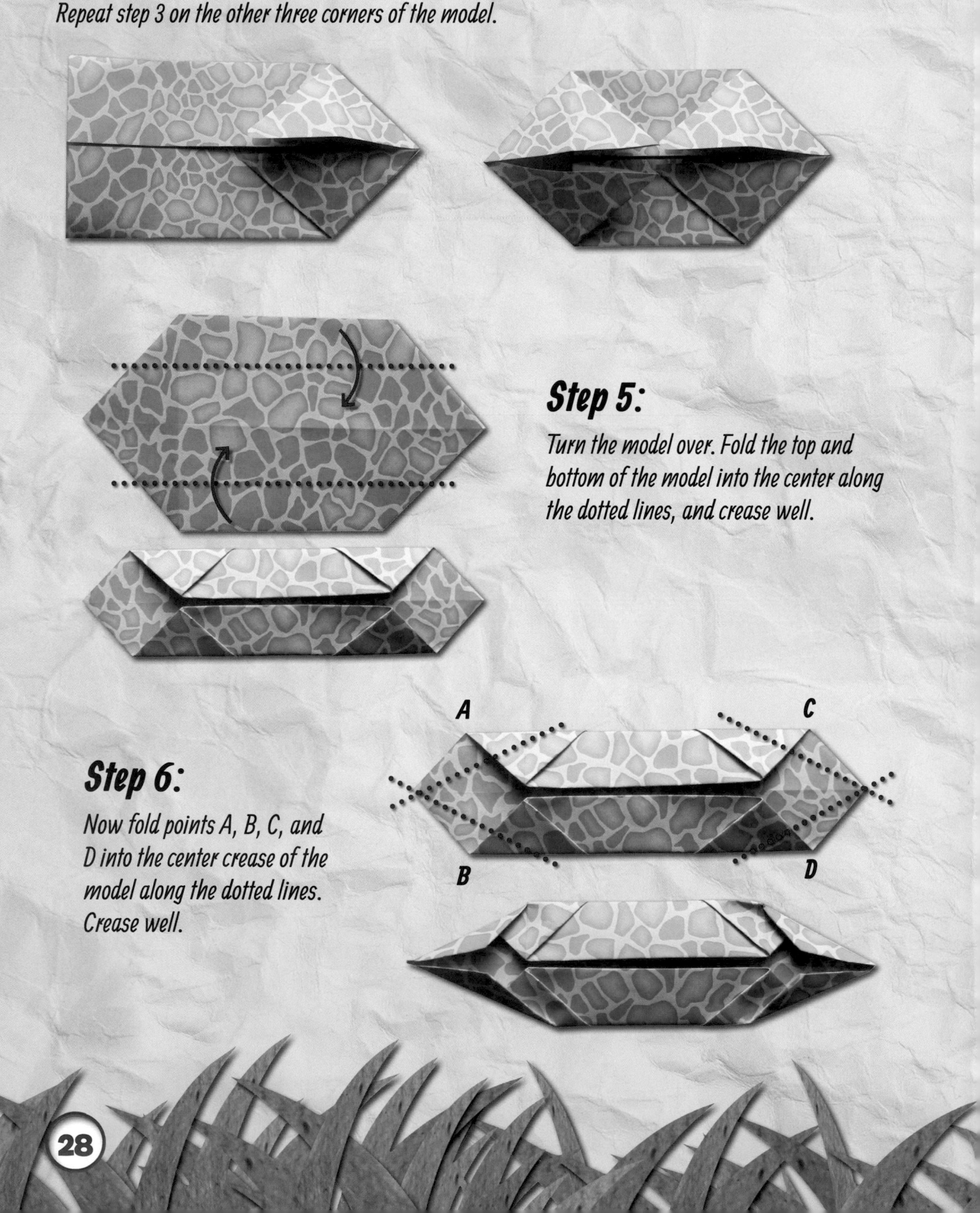

Step 5:

Turn the model over. Fold the top and bottom of the model into the center along the dotted lines, and crease well.

Step 6:

Now fold points A, B, C, and D into the center crease of the model along the dotted lines. Crease well.

A   C

B   D

Step 7:

Next, fold the model in half along the center crease.

Step 8:

Unfold the four small triangles on the sides of the model to make the crocodile's legs.

Legs

Step 9:

Finally, draw eyes and jagged teeth on one end of the model.

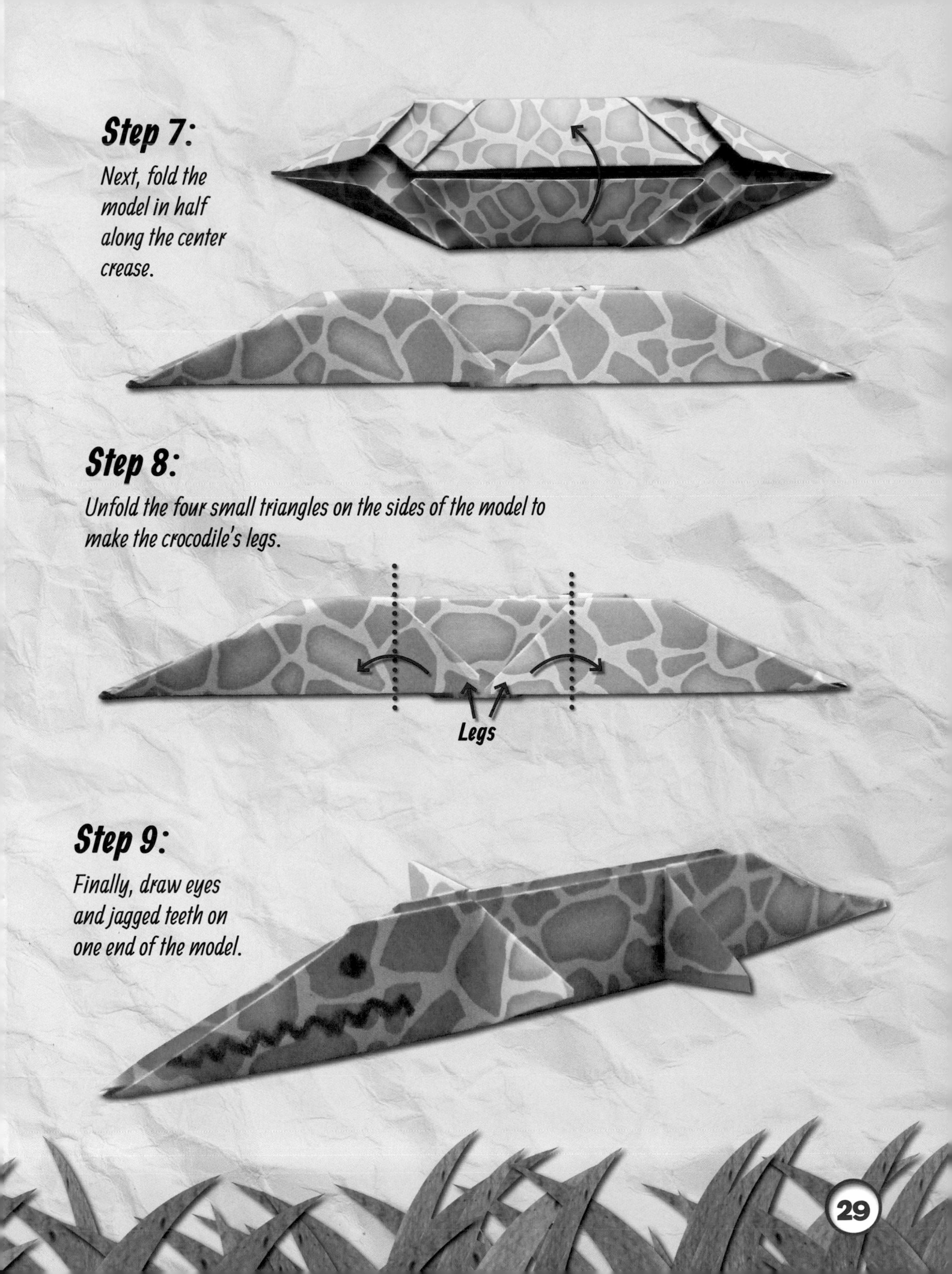

Glossary

bulbs (BUHLBZ)
Round, underground parts of some plants. A bulb stores food for the plant that is growing above ground.

burrows (BUR-ohs)
Underground homes used by animals. Some animals dig their own burrows, others use natural holes in the ground or the old, empty burrows of other animals.

grasslands (GRAS-landz)
A hot habitat with lots of grass and few trees or bushes. Sometimes it is very dry, and at other times there is lots of rain.

grazing (GRAY-zing)
Feeding on grass and other plants.

habitat (HA-buh-tat)
The place where an animal or plant normally lives. A habitat may be a grassland, the ocean, or a backyard.

herds (HURDZ)
Groups of animals. A herd may be made up of animals from the same family or be a group of unrelated animals that live together for company and safety.

impressive (im-PREH-siv)
Having size, physical qualities, or skills that make others admire you.

matriarch (MAY-tree-ark)
A female who leads a family, or group. She is normally the oldest and most experienced member of the group.

origami (or-uh-GAH-mee)
The art of folding paper to make small models. Origami has been popular in Japan for hundreds of years. It gets its name from the Japanese words *ori*, which means "folding," and *kami*, which means "paper."

predators (PREH-duh-turz)
Animals that hunt and kill other animals for food.

prey (PRAY)
An animal that is hunted by another animal as food.

prides (PRYDZ)
Groups, or families, of lions.

reptiles (REP-tylz)
Animals such as snakes, lizards, turtles, crocodiles, and alligators that are cold-blooded and have scaly skin.

trunks (TRUNGKZ)
The long body parts of elephants that are a combined nose and upper lip.

tusks (TUSKZ)
Long, pointed teeth that grow outside of the mouth.

unique (yoo-NEEK)
One of a kind.

For web resources related to the subject of this book, go to:
www.windmillbooks.com/weblinks
and select this book's title.

Read More

Allgor, Marie. *Endangered Grassland Animals*. New York: PowerKids Press, 2013.

Haywood, Karen. *Crocodiles and Alligators*. New York: Cavendish Square, 2010.

Shea, Mary Molly. *Lions*. New York: Gareth Stevens, 2011.

Index